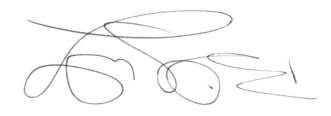

www.covenantpublishing.com

COVENANT
P U B L I S H I N G

P.O. Box 390 Webb City, Missouri 64870
Call toll free at 877.673.1015

Library of Congress Cataloging-in-Publication Data
Wilson, Billy, 1964-.
  Zuzu's petals : our wonderful life with God / Billy Wilson.
    p. cm.

  ISBN 1-892435-46-2 (hardcover)
  1. Christian life. I. Title.
   BV4501.3W554 2004
   248.4—dc22
                              2004001093

Zuzu's Petals

Our Wonderful Life with God

Billy Wilson

COVENANT
PUBLISHING

Dedication

In recognition of their vast contribution to my life, this first book of mine can only be dedicated to Coventry and Caroline Wilson. Ma Da and ma wee Maw.

My Dad used to say to me, *"You never miss the water till the well runs dry."* He never spoke a truer word. I would trade a year of my life for another day with him. Thank God he obeyed the gospel. Now the days will stretch into eternity.

My Mum is, as she has always been, the glue that holds the family together. In the face of many a trial her faith has spoken more clearly than any sermon I've ever heard, or could ever hope to preach.

Hopefully this little book will go some way to prove I listened to some of what they had to say.

Table of Contents

The seeker enters the
spiritual arena full of doubt,
mixed with a touch of anxiety,
only to exit filled with
a confidence of God's love
that can only come from above.

Foreword

How would you like a bit of chocolate? Billy Wilson has a way, doesn't he? His personality is a mixture of a mild Sunday on a park bench and an electrical storm. While it is quite easy to enjoy the man, one can never rest for what has yet to be said will rock your socks . . . in a good way, understand.

Zuzu's Petals is such a combination. The book is a charmer. But just as there are those hiding behind big rocks poised to jump out and scare the daylights out of you, all in fun of course, get ready for Billy's verbal surprises that will pop out and give you resurgent delight. You'll both enjoy the book and learn.

Any who would like to reclaim the core of the gospel in nugget form, *Zuzu's Petals* is for you. The words make sense to the hungry and burdened spirit. The thing I like best about what Billy has written is that it gives any who have felt beaten and defeated by life's rudeness a clear reason to think there may be a ray of hope. The stuffy and smug attend church only to leave more stuffy . . . more smug. The seeker enters the spiritual arena full of doubt, mixed with a touch of anxiety, only to exit filled with a confidence of God's love that can only come from above.

Zuzu's Petals addresses the possibility of a most Wonderful Life. Good for you, Billy Wilson. You have given counties and continents reason to renew the heart. Who wouldn't want to share such a bit of chocolate?

Terry Rush
author of
The Miracle of Mercy

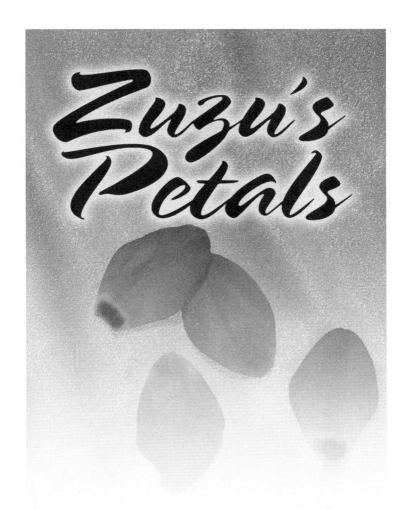

Zuzu's Petals

CHAPTER 1

In the beginning . . .

Abundant life
is the only kind of
life God knows.

GOD CREATED. . . .

About a quarter of a mile long, located on the West Coast of Scotland at Wemyss Bay is a rock formation. The fishing isn't as good as it used to be, but even then was never terrific. However, it affords a view of creation that is just splendid. On my last visit the mackerel chose to visit relations elsewhere and left me to enjoy fishing's close cousin, peaceful relaxation.

It was a glorious summer's day, the sun dancing on the water, the silence periodically broken by the sound of the gulls cheering me on in hopes they'd get the fish, and the sound of gentle waves lapping against the rocks. Used to be, when I was younger, any old place on the rocks would do, but I'm 38 now. I was sitting on a Wal-Mart special; what can only be described as an extra large, extra comfortable, extra everything throne. It takes something of the wild edge out of fishing but the older I get the more I welcome these types of things.

Relaxing in the sunshine I cast a lazy glance along the coastline, not focusing on anything but taking in everything. It was after lunchtime and quickening my appetite was the aroma always present at the receding tide. As it bade its farewell it left behind a series of little rock pools. This intrigued me so much I left the comfort of my throne and walked over to one, no bigger than an average size dining table.

There before me was a little self-contained world surrounded by plant life, created by the constant visiting tide. If I was quiet and still for long enough every now and then the inhabitants would reveal themselves. I was, excuse the pun, hooked—well at least something was. There was Mr. Crab, Mr. Limpet, Mr. Starfish and a few other creatures that I had no idea what they were. A little neighbourhood where everyone seemed to know each other—giving each other little waves as they passed by and went about their business. It was like a little soap opera, except this one was worth watching.

As I studied this world within a world it struck me, that every now and then, when the tide would come in, this little world was engulfed by another world. A bigger world, a better world, the depths and wonders it could not possibly fathom. And as pleasant as this little kingdom seemed I couldn't help but feel pity for Mr. Crab and Mr. Limpet. I couldn't help but think they were missing out. I mean, they looked comfortable enough, and no doubt they were, but in comparison to what they could have? Of course, the bigger world offered more dangers but surely these shrink in comparison to the weight of glory revealed there.

In the beginning God created the heavens and the earth . . .

One second into history and God's eternal nature, His benevolent heart, full-to-bursting (and burst) with an eagerness to bless in an out-pouring of divine and holy indulgence, was right there on His sleeve for everyone to see. The void had been filled and space was cluttered with planets, stars, galaxies, quasars and a host of other things we have still yet to discover.

While the ceiling of creation, although mind-blowingly staggering, was barren and bereft of life, the living room itself teemed with it. The sea, a stew of creatures too numerous to list and too splendid to describe. The land, a harmony of animation and a riot of color paraded itself before the eyes of the Almighty and He said, "good." Although initially strangers, each creature occupied their allotted squares, moving as their Creator determined. Above us, a symphony, performed by winged musicians, rang in our ears. What a glorious week that was.

The world had been born and it was ALIVE! And why not? For the creation itself was not a project or an experiment from a thumb-twiddling God with nothing better to do with eternity. It was a natural manifestation emanating from a heart too laden with love and too selfless to keep it to itself— and too alive to be contained. Life extended Himself, heaven exploded and there we were. Or simply put: God opened His heart and we fell out.

The fact we continue to revolve means only that our Father's heart still marches to the same beat. God isn't on a different page or singing from a different song sheet than He was on week one. His heart toward us is still love, and love of the same passion and intensity. When Jesus arrived He continued to sing the chorus of creation, *"I have come that they may have life, and that they may have it more abundantly"* (NKJ).

Abundant life is the only kind of life God knows. One glance at creation ought to make this clear. For Adam was not placed in a window box but in a garden. He wasn't asked to take his place within creation, but to rule over it. And the "good" of Genesis one only became "very good" after his arrival.

Once the stage had been set, and every creature was occupying its place, the command was given, and given to all alike, *"Go forth and multiply."* You see, it wasn't enough for God to have the world alive and fresh, He desired it to be perpetually alive and fresh. That as the days and seasons would roll into the ages, the Masterpiece, with every new birth and every reproduction, would be forever new.

We consider the creation and rightly marvel but I think it's important to note that we now gaze upon a soiled and spoiled earth. Before we entered the scene some six billion people had trampled its courts, and yet it still looks incredible. Prior to our arrival the earth had suffered at the hands of sinful men, and yet, still, it looks marvellous: a bride who has refused to allow the advancing years to detract much from her original beauty. The multiplied sin of at least six millennia of generations has the world been exposed and subjected to, and yet, and yet still,

"The heavens declare the glory of God; the skies proclaim the work of his hand."

That God seeks to bless us is true, although that doesn't really capture it. Adam was deluged by blessings. And I don't know, maybe like children who are born with a silver spoon in their mouths he truly struggled to appreciate it. That's me speculating. But where no speculation is necessary, is understanding that since our fall God has sought to do nothing less with us than He did at first. From that day until now He has, at every opportunity, sought to plough us with goodness, mercy, and grace . . . fill in the blanks.

Tell me, brothers and sisters, why does Mr. Crab, Mr. Limpet and Mr. Starfish from Wemyss Bay seem overly familiar to me? Is it because, too often, we're content with a little self-contained existence when there's something far better out there?

Every now and then what alcoholics refer to as a moment of clarity comes our way, usually during some fine preaching of the word of God, the challenging kind. When this happens we suddenly become aware of a bigger world, a better world, the depths and wonders we could not possibly fathom. We abruptly realize our little comfortable worlds are surrounded by an infinitely superior existence.

I believe that when these moments come we have a choice. We can leave the comfort of what we know for the adventure of a lifetime, following His holy call, or we can remain as we were. But let's ask ourselves this: Why should we be content with a pool when our Father has prepared for us an ocean?

This book is an effort to help us think about our God as He has revealed Himself with regard to the Creation, how He feels about us now, and what He has planned for us in the future. It will hopefully speak to you about the work He is doing among us: renewing us through faith, knowledge and mercy—and finally the renewal of all things.

If you have half the amount of fun reading it as I did writing it then I'll have had double the amount of fun you did.

Catch the tide! Swim brothers and sisters, swim, and discover things about God you never dreamt possible. This, more than anything is the challenge of the book. Enjoy.

Zuzu's Petals

CHAPTER 2

There's more than this

RENEWED THROUGH FAITH (1)

This is what faith does.
It enables us to see what
the faithless cannot,
and what sounds to those
who cannot see as lunacy.

2 Corinthians 4:16

Therefore we do not lose heart.
Though outwardly we are wasting away,
yet inwardly we are being renewed day by day.

He was about as male as we come. He was a man's man: One of those individuals who would never cause us to doubt his sexual leaning and one definitely unfamiliar with his "femininity"—whatever that is. I always imagine him sitting down to a bowl full of nails for breakfast. Samson.

He had his faults, of course, like the rest of us. He loved women, and mimicking the first of our kind foolishly gave into one's tempting pleas. But for all of that he was a man God swore by, remembered and ultimately delivered that fateful morning when a group of Dagon worshipers made the fatal mistake of inviting him along to morning assembly as the featured guest. He went down a treat, a big hit. Raised the roof and brought the house down I seem to recall.

Over and above that, he could always boast that he'd been privileged to meet the most stupid man who ever lived. Have you never wondered to yourself, "What on earth was the 1000th man thinking?" Here are 999 of his fellow soldiers lying dying beneath him and this maniac thinks, "I'll have a go."

But whether it was 999 soldiers and an idiot, whether it

was the town gates, whether it was a lion or two gigantic pillars that stood before him, the man, God bless him, placed his faith on the correct number and spun the wheel—for all his faults.

When it all boils down. When this whole thing boils down, it boils down to this: Faith!

Although love conquers all, faith certainly gives her a run for her money. God is impressed and moved by faith. Only twice do the Gospels record for us that Jesus was amazed, and in both incidents it was because of faith. Once by the lack of it (Mark 6:6), and once by the abundance of it (Luke 7:9).

Faith is a temptation too far for God. He is naturally drawn to it, not only finding it pleasing but altogether irresistible. So much so He decided to hinge our salvation upon it.

I believe what we desperately need to understand about faith is that when it is expressed it is *God's* name that's on the line, *His* reputation. And He has bound Himself in oath to answer its call. God comes flying to the faithful, not to uphold His people (though He does that), but to uphold His *name*. *This* is why we are confident that faith will never be abandoned or neglected. It's not about us; it's about Him!

When God calls us to be faithful we're inclined to wonder what's so special about us that God would respond to our actions? And consequently we decline to act. Well, there's nothing special about us. He doesn't respond to faith for our sakes. He responds because there is something much weightier at stake than our reputations: His word. He responds because He has promised to respond, and He who promises is faithful.

It's not discernment, knowledge or even wisdom that

enables us to blinker the world from our sight, it's faith. (This is why, when we're discouraged from living by sight, the alternative supplied is faith.) Now any one or a combination of these things may accompany her on her journey but faith is the vehicle. Faith is the substance, by which we hear God's call. It allows us to hear the world without actually listening to it. And faith is the battlefield where the world wars with us. For if she defeats us there she wins everything.

I don't particularly enjoy the experience of flying, though I do it a lot. There's just something strangely unnerving about traveling at 500mph, 32,000 feet in the air, in a large aluminium tube. One of the things I find most comforting when flying is my mini-disk player. Above the roar of the engines and the noise created by a few hundred passengers, Babyface, Dean Martin, Stevie Wonder, Mariah Carey or a host of others gather to croon me to sleep, and although I can still hear the plane and the 300 sardines packed inside, I'm no longer listening to them. Though they are undeniably real they might as well be on a different plane.

I recently visited Crete with Margaret. A little village on the southern coast was our chosen destination: Mirtos. Walk two minutes in any given direction and you would be standing outside the little sleepy hollow. Little old Greek ladies, wrapped in their custom black clothing, walked the streets shaking their heads at the scantily clad European visitors. Small gatherings of Greek men would sit on the street corners, sip coffee and discuss soccer—never agreeing with each other. And also, so it seemed, the world's cat convention was there at the time.

It was 8 A.M., and what had quickly become a tradition,

I was strolling my way down to one of the tavernas for break-fast. This time I had my mini-disk player with me, and Stevie Wonder was belting out "Sir Duke," (you know the one . . . "Music is a world within itself, with a language we all under-stand"), and I realized that I had begun to walk with a swag-ger in keeping with the groove Stevie always manages to pro-duce. It was then that I realized the eyes of the Greeks may have been upon me. I had a little laugh to myself and subse-quently returned to a natural stroll. But I found myself think-ing, why isn't everyone grooving to this, and then remem-bered I was the only one hearing the music.

This is how God would have us: In tune with Him, hear-ing only Him and stepping our way down through our streets to His groove. Regardless of the noise around us, whether it is a Boeing 747, 300 passengers or whatever, God would have us set our minds and fix them upon Him.

This world is a fog of noise, with voices coming at us from every corner, pleading with us for our attention. "Own this," "Buy this," "Wear this," Drive this," "Live here," Vacation there," "Believe this," "Follow that." She teaches us to depend on her, deceives us into thinking she's all there is and entices us to believe that the pleasures she has and the comforts she offers are to be valued above all things. She wants us to relax in her surroundings, intoxicated by her indulgences and march to her beat.

Marc Cohn is convinced that if there's a God in heaven He drives a silver Thunderbird, and although I admire his taste I doubt very much that God would be as wide-eyed as we are at such trivialities.

Steve Martin, in *The Jerk*, is having a go at his wife

because all she seems to be interested in is his money. She responds by claiming, *"I'm not interested in the money . . . it's the stuff."* We like our stuff, don't we? Too much, perhaps.

The world bombards us with this type of thing: Commercials, movies, newspapers and magazines, soaps, and advertising. If you sit and think long enough about it, it's deafening—all these voices competing for our attention.

The world does all she can to surround us. Bedlam: begging us, pleading with us, promising to fulfill all our heart's desires. And through the fog she envelops us with, there comes a voice. No louder than any other voice, for it's not the volume that ought to be of interest to us, it's the source. And the voice says, *"There's more. There's more to it than this."*

Even in religion we're not spared from the noise. Worship there, worship here, and join us. We have an orchestra, a choir, a gymnasium, a counselor, twenty different Bible classes; we finish on time and we'll cater to your every need. Bedlam, bedlam, bedlam.

We're attending church now, supposedly the most selfless organization on earth and doing it with the most selfish reasons. What's in it for *us*, or for our children!

Well, who cares what they've got? *"What's their gospel?"* is the question—the only question! Is their gospel the Christ's? Do they love one another? Are they benevolent to the poor? Do they help the weak? Are they compassionate towards strugglers? Are their elders shepherds? Is it a hospital for the spiritually wounded? Are they actively sharing their faith? These are the questions we should be posing, surely.

Faith doesn't only move mountains. It helps us ask the right questions. It enables people to join, or stay with a congregation that perhaps isn't the fanciest in the world. It enables people to serve, and serve humbly. To sit by the bedside of the sick and dying. To remain faithful to a spouse—or forgive a sinful one. It enables churches to contribute more so that the poor around them may eat, to hold fast to the truth in the midst of challenging trends and gospels, to embrace sinners from their community and stand face to face with the criticism that may come their way because of it. And it enables them to rejoice in the gospel, so that there isn't a snowball's chance in hell of them substituting it for something that might look "nicer" or make them "feel better."

Faith enables us to hear the voice. *"There's more. There's more to it than this."*

Encamped around Elisha that morning was the Aramean army, armed to the teeth and all looking in his direction. Next to him, quaking at the knees, and doing his best to resemble an Aramean, no doubt, was his servant Gehazi. He manages to blurt out, *"Oh Lord. What shall we do?"* Hide? Can't; the Arameans know they're there. Fight? Can't; they're outnumbered. Run? Can't; they're surrounded. The question is valid and demands a response. The response comes and is as perplexing as it is swift? *Relax!*

"Don't worry," Elisha gently suggests, and goes on to provide the reasoning behind the madness of the proposition. *"Those who are with us are more than those who are with them."*

Gehazi, undoubtedly wondering if Elisha has a little flask that he doesn't know about, must have resembled Custer's last man. What was to happen next must have made Gehazi feel like a million dollars—that feeling when your older brother arrives just as the bullies close in around you. Elisha prays and Gehazi's eyes are opened to the sight of the army of God (chariots of fire) surrounding the army that is surrounding them. But understand this. **Understand it!** Elisha's prayer didn't call the army of God onto the battlefield, it only made visible what was already there.

This is what faith does. It enables us to see what the faithless cannot, and what sounds to those who cannot see as lunacy. So, ask yourself, What is surrounding you? Cancer? Death? Financial worries? Family troubles? Church problems? Well, have a little prayer and take another look. Go on, I dare you. Can't you see them? Chariots of fire surrounding that which is surrounding you? I hope to God you can. But if you cannot, relax. All faith would do is make visible what is already there.

Faith is irresistible to God. Move in it and prepare for His presence. I mean set a place for Him at your table, for He's coming. And through faith we are being renewed every single day.

So, let the world shout, let it scream in our ears and surround us with a smog of commotion. Let it say everything it wants to say. Then let God speak, and listen closely as He assures us yet again, *"There's more. There's more to it than this."*

CHAPTER 3

Blessed are the lunatics

RENEWED THROUGH FAITH (2)

Make room for God,
is the Biblical request.
For there's a magical land,
lying on the outskirts of sight,
where God Himself dwells, and
He is anxious to meet us there.

1 Corinthians 4:10
We are fools for Christ.

I briefly made mention in the last chapter that faith not only enables us to do many things, but also that it sounds like lunacy to the ears of those around us who find themselves a little short on it. I'd like to pick up that thought now and run with it a little.

While others may be bragging about their new donkey, or the fact that they had been granted Roman citizenship, or anything else worth boasting about in the first century, Paul, in 1 Corinthians 4, lays claim to a most distinguished title among men, *"Fools for Christ."* He elaborates on this peculiar boast by saying. *"To this very hour we go hungry and thirsty, we are in rags, we are brutally treated, we are homeless. We work hard with our own hands. When we are cursed, we bless; when we are persecuted, we endure it; when we are slandered, we answer kindly. Up to this moment we have become the scum of the earth, the refuse of the world."*

God would have us to be at peace with the world, making every effort to live righteously and peaceably among them, if not with them. However, the world, it seems, has always had a tendency to dismiss our advancements. And this is not limited to the Christian era. This has been par for the course since the sacrifice of Abel.

They were many and undoubtedly loud, sneering and patronizing. *"Hey, preacher, what you doing with all the wood?* And then a little later, *"Hey, Stupid! How you going to get the boat to water?"* God bless him, Noah just kept hammering away.

Can't you hear them? Standing, scratching their heads, bewildered and saying to each other, *"Check these lunatics out! They're at it again. Every day for the past week they just keep walking around, and now seven times today. Oh look! This should be good. Looks like they're going to play us a little tune. Ha, ha, ha . . . uh oh . . . hey, what's that rumbling?"*

Or even within the camp. *"We have to what? Stand in a circle, break our jars and blow our trumpets? Is he crazy? He's already sent 31,700 men home because we had 'too many'."*

And these examples could be multiplied many times over. Faith, to the eyes and ears of the faithless is lunacy.

2 Corinthians 5:7
We live by faith, not by sight.

What else can this be but a call to go beyond what we can see? For when we make plans for what we can achieve, where then is our faith, if not simply in ourselves? And someone may well wisely add, *"For do not the pagans do likewise?"*

Make room for God, is the Biblical request. For there's a magical land, lying on the outskirts of sight, where God Himself dwells, and He is anxious to meet us there.

"As the crow flies" must have been the order for the day, for Jesus took a shortcut across the waves that evening, on foot. And after three and a half miles I imagine He was tired so He went to hitch a lift the rest of the way. Or, because He had already taught them how to deal with a storm perhaps He wanted to see if they could handle it without Him.

If I could have a Polaroid of just one instance in the ministry of Jesus, a snapshot of the look on the disciples' faces as they peered over the side of the boat to see Jesus dancing with the waves, would surely be among the contenders.

Being understandably terrified, Jesus calms them down and makes His way over to the boat. But His progress is halted by the voice of a lunatic. *"Lord, if it is you, tell me to come to you on the water."* There isn't a doubt in my mind, if not outwardly, at least inwardly Jesus punched the air in delight. *"Come,"* He said, and Polystyrene Pete, for all his many faults, took his feet from the secure wooden deck of a boat and placed them upon the choppy waters of Galilee—and did it! He did it! The man walked on water! If this doesn't make your toes curl I'm afraid we're going to have to kick the dirt in over you.

This instance in Jesus' ministry is undoubtedly the most overlooked passage in Scripture. Everyone I've heard preach on it, anyone I've read writing about it and all that I've heard comment on it must be wearing blinkers. For without exception they all go on about Jesus. And with all due respect I do my utmost to refrain from shouting, *"So what!"*

Those who know me know I mean no disrespect here. But that Jesus walked on water—so what! I mean, big deal! **He's God!** If Jesus *couldn't* walk on water we'd all be in big trouble and *that* would be the miracle. Look, we have two people walking on water here. One of them is God and the other is a simple, ordinary man, and everyone, and for the life of me I can't figure out why, is more impressed by God doing it.

"Yeah, but he sank!" is normally the response I get when I begin speaking about this. And my response is always the same. Usually I begin by laughing (as I am accustomed to do when talking about this passage—and in fact even as I write I'm laughing here now), and reply, *"No, he didn't sink. He **began** to sink."* There's a world of difference. But even then I have to hold back the rebuke in my speech as I say, *"Even if he did ultimately sink. So what! If he managed just one single solitary step, isn't that itself worthy of righteous envy on our part?"* Or is our faith of such measure that we would have managed more steps than Peter?

"Yeah, but Jesus rebuked him," is a common comeback. And following that, more laughter from me. However, they are, of course, correct. Jesus did rebuke him, and undoubtedly, in doing so, spared some of the blushes of those still safe and secure within the confines of the boat. No doubt, even a couple of them may have sniggered, as big-mouthed Peter got his comeuppance. *"He, He, He,"* I hear them whisper, *"He called Peter 'little faith.'"* I tell you, they're lucky it was Jesus floating (or was it flying?) out there and not me, for I wouldn't have been able to stop there. I would have gone on, and opened both barrels, *"Yes, you're right. I did call him little faith. But you!? Standing there, feet all dry with faithlessness. You have none!"*

Oh it's all so easy, isn't it? To stand safe and secure in our little boats, laughing at those who have the courage to brave the waves, even if they don't have the faith to keep it going for very long. To our shame (and multiplied shame if it does-n't shame us), at least they get out of the boat!

And it's all too easy to laugh as they begin to sink, while remarking to each other how so incredibly wise we were to stay put. But answer me this. Who of the twelve, that day, had their hand in the hand of the Master? Who of the twelve was closest to Jesus? Who of the twelve took his last breath on this earth remembering the day he was master of the elements? And who of the twelve can utter, for all eternity, those tremendous words to Jesus, *"Hey, Jesus, remember the time we took a stroll on the sea?"* That's right, it's the lunatic.

Faith! When it all boils down, it boils down to faith. It has brought fire from the sky, bread from heaven, water from rocks, nations from disaster and so, so much more. Jesus encourag-ingly reported to us that nothing lies beyond its power.

Hebrews chapter 11 has 40 verses, all dealing with the accomplishment of faith. *"By faith [Abel, Enoch, Noah, Abraham, Isaac, Jacob, Joseph, Moses, Rahab, Gideon, Barak, Samson, Jephthah, David, Samuel and the prophets] . . . con-quered kingdoms, administered justice, and gained what was promised; who shut the mouths of lions, quenched the fury of the flames, and escaped the edge of the sword; whose weak-ness was turned to strength; and who became powerful in battle and routed foreign armies. Women received back their dead, raised to life again."*

For thirty-four and a half verses the writer of Hebrews catalogs great men and women and their numerous accom-plishments through faith. However, it's the three and a half verses that follow I'd like to comment on and conclude this section. That is, lest we become disheartened when our faith is not answered in keeping with the previously mentioned greats. Let me include it here to save you finding a Bible:

Hebrews 11:35-38

Others were tortured and refused to be released,
so that they might gain a better resurrection.
Some faced jeers and flogging, while still others
were chained and put in prison.
They were stoned; they were sawn in two;
they were put to death by the sword.
They went about in sheepskins and goatskins,
destitute, persecuted and ill-treated—
the world was not worthy of them.
They wandered in deserts and mountains,
and in caves and holes in the ground.

You see, while it's true that faith accomplished so many things and has delivered so many from so much, it is equally true that the very same faith delivered others into nothing more than torture, jeering, flogging and imprisonment; stoning, banishment and death.

The question is not, *"where will our faith lead us?"* It's simply a question of *"will we have it, regardless of where it leads us?"* Whether we conquer kingdoms with it or whether we're tortured because of it is neither here nor there. That's for God to decide. What is for us to decide is whether or not we'll have it and act upon it.

In *Phenomenon*, George Malley (John Travolta) is trying desperately to win over the love of Lace (Kyra Sedgwick). She's already been bitten and left with two children so he has his work cut out for him.

Lace makes chairs out of branches; nice to look at but highly uncomfortable. George buys his friends some but he's bought so many his house becomes a storehouse for them. Later on in the movie, Bains (someone who has just lost his own sweetheart, Lisa, again) is having a go at George. This is too much for an eavesdropping friend of George's (Doc; Robert Duvall), so he picks up the gauntlet in his defence.

"Bains, how's your lady love?" asks the Doc.

"We broke up."

"Really. That's too bad. Now George, he's got a love by his side and she's sticking with him. You know why? Because he bought her chairs. You ever buy Lisa's chairs?

"God, Doc's really drunk tonight."

"Every woman has her chairs, Bains. You ever find out what Lisa's chairs were and buy some?"

You want to know what God's chairs are? Faith . . . hope and love. And our lives ought to be storehouses full of them.

So, permit yourself a little lunacy every now and then. Remember what Jesus said, *"Blessed are the lunatics, for they shall inherit the asylum."*

Two men went fishing. One man was an experienced fisherman, the other wasn't. Every time the experienced fisherman caught a big fish, he put it in his ice chest to keep it fresh. Whenever the inexperienced fisherman caught a big fish, he threw it back. The experienced fisherman watched this go on all day and finally got tired of seeing this man waste good fish. "Why do you keep throwing back all the big fish you catch?" he asked. The inexperienced fisherman replied, "I only have a small frying pan" (Dwayne Savaya).

Let's not laugh at the joke and then go right on ahead with small frying pans. Let's not wait for God to throw us smaller fish when we should be buying bigger pans.

The challenge of this little section is simply this: Let us leave the safety of the boat, for Jesus is out there and is desperate to meet us. Let us, with our hands in the hand of the Master, brave the waves and tolerate the sniggering of the faithless. Let us consider those who found their way into Hebrews eleven, see what they saw and so act as they did. And let us do all of this with increased faith, more than they did, because of the closing verse of the chapter.

> *God had planned something better*
> *for us so that only together with us*
> *would they be made perfect.*

CHAPTER 4

I saw God today

RENEWED THROUGH KNOWLEDGE (1)

When we read through Hebrews 11, and that roll call of those who excelled in faith, what we don't find are people acting because of how they felt in any given situation, but rather people acting because of what they knew.

I saw God today and I didn't run away.
I saw the green tree against the blue sky.
I saw the brown tree trunk against the short-cut grass.
I stood on the sodden wet green field
Wet with days of rain.
I looked up and I saw the sun once again,
Hot, burning warm on my face.
I saw the murky pond, browny-grey.
It was teaming with life as I walked away.
I felt the wind blow across the park land.
It caught in the trees and danced
From branch to branch, as the tree it teased.
I saw God today and I didn't run away.
There was a boy playing football;
A dog without a lead;
Children shouting on a roundabout at speed;
An old woman sitting, chatting away to a friend she once
    knew,
Long gone away.
I saw God today and I didn't run away.

(Charles Kennedy: Glasgow, Scotland)

To see God where others can't see Him, to hear Him when others struggle to hear anything and to be assured of His love when others feel cold, takes faith. But where do we find faith? How shall we obtain it, this precious of all jewels?

To listen to some people you could get the impression that faith is some sort of fairy dust or magic potion that works on its own meritorious or esoteric system, choosing at will or at random who it will or will not land on. Paul had this to say about it.

Romans 10:17

So then faith comes by hearing, and hearing by the word of God (NKJ).

Margaret just loves *The Wizard of Oz*, though it takes some badgering to provoke compliments from me for the movie. The reason for this is that as a child I remember feeling robbed by the movie, and on three occasions. The first was when Toto pulled back the curtain to reveal the "wizard." I was more disappointed than Dorothy was when the faker was revealed. The second occasion was when the "wizard" starting handing out the so-called "rewards" for their expedition. And I felt most cheated when Glinda told Dorothy that she could have gone home anytime. I thought, "WHAT!?" You'll remember that her message to Dorothy was that she always had the power, all she had to do was utilize it. That just didn't do it for me. I wanted a real wizard and a fair reward for the travelers.

As I've grown older, and come to realize the significance behind the script, I've mellowed a little, even if I still kick my feet a little at the end of the movie.

There's nothing magical about faith, in that there's nothing mysterious about it. If we want it then it's there for us, and

we've had the ability all along. And kicking ag~
that faith is some kind of fairy dust that chooses to ~
upon a select few, is the above passage from Romans~

Faith comes to us through the word of God, and throu~
request from God Himself (James 1:5, understanding that this
would not be restricted to wisdom). So then, we come to
realize that faith is not only heart-based, but head-based.
That, to some degree, it's an intellectual pursuit.

Now, those of you who are like me, certainly not a heavy-
weight in the brains department, will be pleased to know that
the intellectual pursuit is not one of insurmountable propor-
tions—at all! Certainly there are many areas of Scripture that
have us all scratching our heads, but the fundamentals, the
basics, the staple diet of it all is fruit already fallen from the
tree. And really, all that is required of us is that we go over,
pick it up, and eat—and who couldn't manage that?

God has never been slow to use the ordinary to display His
extraordinary power. In fact, He seems to take quite a delight
in it, littering His book with example after example. There's got
to be something said for the masses who followed after Jesus,
who by and large were simple ordinary folk, while the masses
of the "knowledgeable" stayed home. Or as Mr. Lincoln put it,
"God must love ordinary people. He made so many of them."

We all have our personal struggles and demons to con-
tend with, and this would be true regardless of the amount of
faith we possess. But I am just altogether convinced that we
take more beatings than God intends simply because we
don't have the faith to fight. And we don't have the faith to
fight because, too often, we neglect His word.

Getting to know God is anything but intellectually chal-

·nging. Knowledge, from a Biblical perspective is not gained by intelligence or measured by it. The blessing of seeing God is for the pure in heart according to Jesus. The author of Psalm 119 makes mention that he has more understanding than the elders *because he obeys* God's precepts (v. 100).

Paul says, *". . . our new self is being renewed in* knowledge *of its Creator"*, but we don't have to be Mensa candidates to attain it.

When we read through Hebrews 11, and that roll call of those who excelled in faith, what we don't find are people acting because of how they *felt* in any given situation, but rather people acting because of what they *knew*.

David didn't decide to level the Philistine because a generous portion of "fairy dust" randomly overwhelmed him. Neither did he choose to launch his missile because he *felt* God was with him. There was nothing emotional about this. Well, perhaps there was, but it didn't get a mention in his explanation of it all. When David appeared before Saul he laid out an *argument*.

He said, *"Look Saul. I'm a shepherd. This is what I do. I see off predators. And the Lord who consistently delivers me from lions and bears will do the same here."* The notion that God would save David's father's sheep through him, but Who, at the same time would allow His own flock to perish never entered his mind.

Judges 20:16, has this to say,

Among all these soldiers there were seven hundred chosen men who were left-handed, each of whom could sling a stone at a hair and not miss.

It's an insight to David's skill in this area when we see him taking only five stones. Either that or he knew Goliath had four brothers.

What I can't appreciate are those who talk about this event as though David had never used a sling in his life, and that this approach to battle was a whim, a step into the unknown. You would therefore be compelled to conclude that had God not been present that day the chances of David downing the giant would have been slim-to-none. This is nonsense. What we find going on here is a combination of two things. David's ultimate trust in God, but added to this was his unswerving belief in the talent God had *already* given him with the sling.

The fact that David would have spent years practicing the sling is neither here nor there; the gift (as are all good gifts) was from God. Something we'd do well to remember. Regardless of the effort we put in, or the hours we spend in study, or the years of mind-numbing practice to get to where we are in whatever field we sit, the gifts we have are from God. Our earning potential is from Him.

The God who sat by David's side for years while he fended off bears and lions was the same God David took into battle with him. I am firmly persuaded that God didn't carry that stone as it left the sling. I'm saying the shot was David's, though I hasten to add that the skill David had acquired was from God in the first place. The Goliath incident wasn't simply an exhibition of David's faith in God, but also, and equally so, a demonstration of his knowledge *of* God in the ability He had already blessed him with.

Therefore, we need to understand that *this* is what we're

called to. Not only a belief and trust in God but also a call to use what he has *already* given us, for His glory. The parable of the talents is clear: No one starts with a dud hand. There are only those who use what they already have and those who bury what they already have.

Samson was blind, but even a blind man knows when he needs a haircut. Samson's returning locks spoke clearly, and reminded him of a God that was faithful to His promises. He acted upon what he knew about God.

It's not always true that as our knowledge of God increases our faith does too, but it is true that those who become more faithful are those who increase their knowledge about God. We cannot have faith in something we know nothing about. Would you fly in a plane made out of spaghetti? Would you walk over a paper bridge? Would you drive a car built from balsa wood? No, you would do none of these, and the reason is because you lack the faith necessary to gamble your life on such perishable material. And the reason you lack the faith is because of your knowledge of these materials. It's not a question of how we feel about it. Feelings are determined by what we know. Thus as our knowledge of God increases then so should our faith.

Jonah didn't attempt to take his two weeks' vacation cruising around the Mediterranean because he didn't like Assyrians (though he didn't like the Assyrians). He fled from Nineveh because of what he *knew* about God. He knew that God was compassionate and would be merciful to Nineveh if they repented, so he figured the best way to combat this would be to refuse to give them the message in the first place. Of course God would have none of this and thus determined that if Jonah was adamant about this spring break the least He could do for His prophet was to ensure that he had a whale of a time.

All the Greats of Hebrews 11 acted in this way. Not because they awoke one morning covered in the magic powder, but because they believed in, trusted and *knew* their God.

The little poem at the beginning of this chapter is not only a fine reflection of a man I have come to know as having the ability to see God where others seem to labor; it's a challenge for us to do likewise. But how will we ever see God if we don't know what He looks like? And how will we ever determine what He looks like if we don't spend time looking at His self-portrait—the Word?

Let us get to *know* God by knowing *about* God. Then we'll see Him where others cannot, hear Him when others struggle, and feel the warmth of His love regardless of the chills of winter. When we do that, the last thing we'll do, surely, is run away.

CHAPTER 5

Let the ballerina dance

RENEWED THROUGH KNOWLEDGE (2)

The Author of authors
only wrote one book.
Though featuring a
cast of millions,
and many of them
great men and women,
He Himself is the Hero.

It's hardly surprising she dances. You would too if you were cooped up in a box for days or weeks at a time. So, every time the lid is lifted on one of those old-fashioned jewelry boxes the music sounds and the little ballerina just springs into life.

I would surmise the original designer of the musical jewelry box had more in mind than just a gimmick. I'm certain that more thought went into this than simply an angle to shift them from the shelves. The reason I am convinced about this is because of the contents of the box. Although a woman may keep everything but the kitchen sink inside her purse, and even then only because it won't fit, her jewelry box is especially different.

A woman's jewelry box is a sanctuary, a Holy of Holies. Treasured within its walls are her most valued belongings: things that are perhaps not only, or even, expensive but that are just all in all irreplaceable. *This* is why it is so fitting that a ballerina dances and music plays when she opens it, and why I am convinced the designer had more in mind than simply a marketing ploy.

When the King walked on stage it was to Sprach Zarathustra (*2001 A Space Odyssey*), and rightly so. Most careful thought always goes into the choosing of the music that accompanies a bride on her walk down the aisle. Scottish comedian, Billy Connelly, says that the Queen thinks the world smells like new paint, because ten feet in front of her there's a couple of painters making sure her surroundings are proper. She never arrives anywhere without an appropriate fuss, indeed a fanfare. And God Himself has determined that the opening of every new day should begin with a song. And on cue, every single morning, just as the sun begins his ascent into our skies they are filled with the melodies of nature.

No one complains about these things, because it is fitting for our most cherished possessions, people and ceremonies to be greeted in such a manner. This is why when we lift the lid on the Word of God we really ought to be hearing the music. When our fingers fumble their way over the sacred score there really ought to be a symphony, if not a fanfare. Those with ears to hear and eyes to see don't simply read about the individuals in the book. When they open the lid they see them dance. For inside this particular box are our most treasured possessions. We open it and find a God madly in love with His creation, a God who proved to us that He loved us more than He loved life itself. We find treasure that permeates our hearts with a warmth so comforting that the Author Himself becomes to us irresistible.

The Author of authors only wrote one book. Though featuring a cast of millions, and many of them great men and women, He Himself is the Hero. Through millennia of adventures He rode saving all that would come to Him. Death was the enemy that stalked us, terrifying us by his presence, until one day *He* strolled into town. On a hill just outside Jerusalem He challenged death to a duel. Death won and the sun hid his face. However, as Death was basking in his triumph the Author was putting the last remaining touches to the final chapter. In English it reads, *"It is finished."* What He really said was, *"I'll be back!"* What a book! The Psalmist had this to say about it:

Psalm 19:7-10

The law of the LORD is perfect,
reviving the soul.
The statutes of the LORD are trustworthy,
making wise the simple.
The precepts of the LORD are right,
giving joy to the heart.
The commands of the LORD are radiant,
giving light to the eyes.
The fear of the LORD is pure,
enduring forever.
The ordinances of the LORD are sure
and altogether righteous.
They are more precious than gold,
than much pure gold;
they are sweeter than honey,
than honey from the comb.

Joyful, more precious than gold and sweeter than honey. This is how it should be. This is how we ought to view the word of God. This is the kind of outlook that keeps a layer of dust from ever forming on our Bibles. And this, more than anything, will save us from ever entering the two extremes we find more and more people straying into: either worshiping the book above the Author or neglecting it altogether.

We've already discussed that we lose some battles

because of a lack of faith. I've offered that this lack of faith often results because we neglect His word. Now I'm suggesting a reason as to why we may neglect His word.

Our view of Scripture is of critical importance. For that, more than anything else will determine how often we pick it up, and how enthusiastically we read it.

More precious than gold? Really? Is this our perception of the revealed Word? Can we, with hand on heart honestly say that we value it as more precious than gold? Are we found seeking it with as much enthusiasm as we do, say, our finances? Are we teaching our children that *their* efforts toward God and His word should exceed that of their educational endeavours, and reward them accordingly? Do we invest in Scripture, financially as well as hourly, so that our homes become an environment where not only dwells the quest for God, but that the practical elements are also there to satisfy the thirst?

Jesus said, *"Seek first his kingdom and his righteousness."* First. First in relation to the time we have, the finances He has blessed us with and as our number one priority. God won't settle for second best. Never has. He won't even settle for joint first. All pearls are to be sold and the entire field is to be purchased in order to obtain the greatest prize of all. More precious than gold? Really?

David, for all his faults, understood the value, at least when he wrote this Psalm. He goes on, *"sweeter than honey, than honey from the comb."* Is this really how it tastes to us?

We can pick up a Bible almost anywhere, for almost nothing. Maybe that has contributed to our familiarity with it. But, as the old saying goes, surely we need to guard against familiarity breeding contempt.

We peruse the Bibles in any given bookstore, and depending on the translation, the decoration, included comments and helps, size of print and the publisher we see a host of varying prices. Anything from $5 to $100. When our Father considers the cost of a Bible He sees, not a price tag, but rather the life of His Son and thousands of His people, who, down through the ages, were invested into bringing it to us. If God Himself could price the Bible, and if He did so in keeping with true cost of production, can you imagine what He could charge?

I'll say it again. Our view of Scripture is of critical importance. For that, more than anything else will determine how often we pick it up, and how enthusiastically we read it.

In the movie *Awakenings,* Robert De Niro plays a man (Leonard) plagued by post-Encephalitic syndrome. It's an illness that begins resembling Parkinson's Disease but which completes its work by overpowering its victims into a permanent trance-like state.

While Leonard's on the road to recovery, he meets a girl, and falls for her. But then the medicine stops working and he returns to what he was before. *"Grotesque"* he describes himself as—and he's not far wrong. His entire body twitches uncontrollably yet he still has the wits about him to be aware of it.

He plans to meet the girl one last time to say his final good-bye. He pulls himself together for one final effort, twitches his way to her table and bids his farewell. He leaves the table and leaves her behind, twitching as he goes. Then from out of nowhere he feels a hand on his waist, and then another hand taking his other hand. It's the girl, and she begins, with no music at all, to dance with him, and all his twitchings subside.

Isn't it amazing that there are those who can open the Bible and to no music at all dance their life away and on into heaven itself? Or is it more amazing that there are those who can open it and hear nothing, and treat it no better than the morning newspaper? Worse! At least they read the newspaper.

In *K-19—The Widow-Maker*, two Soviet submarine personnel are lying in their bunks. One of them is looking a little down and his friend asks, *"What's the matter?"*

"I miss seeing the trees, the sun," he sighs.

The response from his comrade? *"You get used to living underwater."*

There's our problem, right there. Too many of us are used to living underwater. The days when we'd lift the Bible with unparalleled enthusiasm, if they were ever there at all, have long since been laid to rest. It's no longer the music to our ears it used to be. We've become accustomed to it, overly familiar with it and treat it like an old car, useful; but something's replaced it.

Let us get back to where we were without swinging into the other extreme and favoring the text over the Author. Let us strive to see what David saw: something more precious than gold and sweeter than honey from the comb.

Wouldn't it be nice if someone designed a Bible where upon opening it a ballerina would dance and a melody played? Wouldn't it be nicer for us not to need that at all? To need nothing like that, for in our hearts, as the words are read we feel a hand around our waist and drift softly into a world where our souls are satisfied as with the choicest of foods?

CHAPTER 6

I would be delighted

RENEWED THROUGH MERCY (1)

Mercy is to our soul
what oxygen is to our lungs,
essential, if we want to
breathe spiritually.
Mercy is what brushes
the dust from us and
gives us motivation
to have another go.

Titus 3:4-6

But when the kindness and love of God our Savior
appeared, he saved us, not because of righteous things
we had done, but because of his mercy.
He saved us through the washing of rebirth
and renewal by the Holy Spirit,
whom he poured out on us generously
through Jesus Christ our Savior. . . .

He found us naked in the garden, rebellious and fallen, and made us clothes. He found us in an ark, hopelessly drifting and produced for us land. He found us slaves in Egypt and granted us freedom. He found us wandering, hungry and thirsty in the wilderness and provided us with direction, food and water. He found us in a land not our own, jumping to Babylonian command and brought us restoration. And now He finds us in dire need of mercy and provides it as abundantly as He always has. He found and He gave. It's the way it is. It's the way it's always been. It's the way it will remain.

We don't meet God on equal footing: A lesson we learned a while back at the bush when the song for the day was "Nothing on my feet I bring." We come to God with cap in hand—nothing to barter or bargain with, nothing to negotiate with. Anything we do possess He gave to us in the first place. So it is as the old song's modern counterpart suggests,

"Nothing in my hand I bring. Simply to thy cross I cling."

Micah says, **"Who is a God like you, who pardons sin and forgives the transgression of the remnant of his inheritance? You do not stay angry for ever but delight to show mercy"** (7:18).

I am no stranger to delight. I sit in a football stadium on a bi-weekly basis that houses almost 60,000 die-hard soccer fans, and every time that little ball stretches the back of the net I witness firsthand exactly what delight is—60,000-fold.

Several weeks ago our national team played Germany in the European qualifiers. The only ticket I could obtain was situated in among the German support. As I took my seat a little apprehensively, getting a taste of Daniel's experience, Germany opened the scoring to the joy of those immediately around me. Hard to take at the best of times but surrounded in such a way I prayed for the ground to open and swallow me. But then it happened. Within seconds of the Germans quieting down somewhere in the stadium rang a single solitary voice piercing the atmosphere with the opening words of "Flower of Scotland." Then another joined in, and another, and another until our national stadium was rocking to the sound and awash with Lion Rampant's and St. Andrews flags proudly waving. It would have brought a tear to a glass eye. I smiled, now thankful for my ticket allocation as I realized what Robert Burns spoke of in *To a Louse*,

> "O wad some Pow'r the giftie gie us
> To see oursels as others see us."

I was both privileged and proud to witness what we look

like from the opposition's point of view, and particularly so *because* we were, at that moment, being defeated. A rare glimpse, perhaps, into the spirit of my nation who have so bravely fought so frequently against the odds. I turned to the German guy sitting next to me and in pigeon English said, "This is what we're like when we're getting beat. You want to see us when we win." I didn't have long to wait for my point to be proven. Scotland scored and Hampden erupted with a display that made Mount St. Helen's look like a burp. I was on the way down after jumping from my seat before I realized where I was. Thankfully at that time the Germans still thought they would go on to win and humored me. I'm no stranger to delight.

Delight is exceeding joy. It is an overwhelming rush of enthusiastic exultation—a cannot-stay-seated, cannot-be-contained breed of passion. And it is *exactly* how God feels whenever He is requested to grant mercy. He is far from the Divine Ebenezer many expect and even proclaim Him to be; sitting in heaven selfishly guarding His mercy like some kind of heavenly banker doling it out under great duress.

When a broken spirit and repentant heart finds its way to the throne of grace it doesn't hear, *"You again?"* or *"How many times?"* or even *"Okay, but this is the last."* It is greeted with the words, *"My child, I would be **delighted** to."*

Mercy is to our soul what oxygen is to our lungs, essential, if we want to breathe spiritually. Mercy is what brushes the dust from us and gives us motivation to have another go. It is precisely what enables us to "forget what lies behind and press on." For if God Himself can find it to forgive us with the hope and expectation that we can "do better," who are we to disagree?

Peter approached Jesus one day, most probably hoping to impress, and asked Him how often he ought to be merciful toward his brother. *"Seven times?"* he suggested. Jesus responded by saying, *"I do not say to you, up to seven times, but up to seventy times seven* (NASB).

Our response to mercy will be dealt with in the next chapter, but for now let's allow ourselves the luxury of the implication of this verse.

Seventy times seven equals four hundred and ninety and works out to once every three minutes in any one day. Jesus is not giving us license to hold the four-hundred and ninety-first sin against anyone. The marvel of the verse is that Jesus is not seeking to be taken literally, not because the number is too large, but because it's too small. What the Lord *is* saying is that He doesn't care how many times we are sinned against, when an appeal for mercy confronts us we grant it; immediately, freely and as frequently as requested. Now, why would He instruct us in this fashion? Well, for a few reasons, but I believe the top contender is because people will judge our God by our actions, and the number one lesson He desires them to learn is that there is mercy to be found in Him.

The implication of the verse, preceded by a small pop quiz, is this. Who is more compassionate, the Lord or us? Who is more forgiving, the Lord or us? Who is more gracious, the Lord or us? Obviously it's the Lord. Well, if the Lord is more compassionate, forgiving and gracious than we are, and He fully expects *us* to forgive so freely and frequently, what does that say about *Him*? Surely He isn't requiring from us a depth of mercy that He Himself isn't willing to at least match. Surely, although on the face of it He seems to be asking a lot of us, He Himself is able and willing to go even beyond this.

I've had some bad days in my life when it comes to sin, and I've had some *really* bad days, but never, I'm sure, have I ever approached Him for mercy four-hundred and ninety times. Isn't it just mind blowingly staggering that even if I had then mercy would have been mine, and the granting of it would have delighted Him as much on the four-hundred and ninetieth time as it did the first? No wonder Micah opens this verse with the words, "Who is like You?"

A while back I heard about a minister who was struggling with a particular problem and openly appealed for the brethren to pray for him, and in particular the elders of the congregation, obviously with James 5:16 in mind. Unfortunately, the *real* problem this preacher had was over-estimating the "shepherds'" Christlikeness. Following the service the elders met with the man and instantly fired him. I thought to myself, sarcastically of course, *"Yeah, that's like Jesus."* Not an ounce of compassion, not a whisper of sympathy. No love, no gentleness of spirit and definitely no concern for the sinner whatsoever.

When I hear about such things, which, thank God isn't too often, my response is always the same; thank goodness it's not them who occupy the throne. What a woeful affair life would be if when we sinned our God came against us like this, and what a prospect of eternal misery, spending forever in the presence of someone like that. Quite frankly, I'd rather have hell.

What on earth prompts these people, who, week in— week out, hear about compassion, forgiveness, grace, sympathy and mercy, to act in such a fashion in the face of sinners? Or *is* that the problem—they're not hearing it?

Maybe their concern was the surrounding area. Maybe their fear was how it would look to the eyes of the local community. And one could hardly blame them. I mean, what would the neighborhood think if they knew a *sinner* was preaching in that particular congregation? God forbid they ever hear that the church is in the business of forgiving people. Yes, fire him and save the church's reputation. For the last thing we desire to be known for, surely, is mercy!

As a community of sinners, albeit forgiven, we sometimes seem to have a dreadful passion for trying to promote to the communities around us the idea that we're anything but. I don't know, but maybe that's why they don't come in. Why would they? Sick people go to a hospital because they want to be cured. Sinners congregate where they'll find mercy, not ridicule. And it's not a question of going "easy on sin." No one was harder on sin than Jesus Himself, and yet sinners surrounded him. Jesus' teaching on sin drew sinners to Him. We have to ask ourselves, does ours?

On the very same day I heard about a different minister caught up in a quite public sin. The following Sunday the elders turned up bright and early and handed each and every Christian, as they walked through the door, a stone. Also, on public television they were interviewed, and stated for all to hear that they would be standing by their minister. *THAT'S IT!* Right there. If God ever stands and applauds, it's reserved for moments such as this. Moments when we identify with the sinner, and though the mob around us is armed with stones, place ourselves, for their sake, in the firing line.

Brothers and sisters, we cannot allow the failings of some to convince us that our God has anything but delight in His heart when we appeal to Him for mercy. He's still in the stone-handing-out business.

In reference to the woman who turned up unannounced, unexpectedly and unwelcome at Simon the Pharisee's house, Bernard had this to say,

"Thanks to thee, most blessed sinner: Thou hast shown the world a safe enough place for sinners—the feet of Jesus, which spurn none, reject none, repel none, and receive and admit all. Where alone the Pharisee vents not his haughtiness, there surely the Ethiopian changes his skin, and the leopard his spots."

There's a verse in the Hebrew letter that could melt an iceberg.

Hebrews 2:11

> ***Both the one who makes men holy***
> ***and those who are made holy***
> ***are of the same family.***
> ***So Jesus is not ashamed***
> ***to call them brothers.***

We find a sinner in a pulpit, or anywhere else for that matter, and are tempted to distance ourselves from them just in case anyone gets the wrong idea about us. Thinking, in our blind stupidity, that this would be the right thing to do. Thinking that we'd be saving someone's reputation, perhaps even God's. Jesus finds sinners and unashamedly sets up camp with them. Not only identifying with them in their weaknesses but willing to be identified with them, period.

Crying all over His feet, in the house of a Pharisee, and surrounded by the "holy" society of Israel, she pleads for mercy. All eyes are on the Christ. "Doesn't He know what kind of woman this is?" is the question. While everyone around is shocked that He would associate Himself with such a low life, He Himself is utterly delighted, only taking a momentary break from it to rebuke the sad, shallow and pathetic theology that would motivate anyone to have anything but compassion on her.

One question shall suffice to close this chapter. Sinners surrounded Jesus and they found delight in each other's company, one side because they were granted mercy and the other because He could afford it. The question? Who surrounds you and what do they find when they do?

CHAPTER 7

Labeled with love

RENEWED THROUGH MERCY (2)

We don't convince people
of their need of forgiveness
by shouting about their sin.
We convince them by
showing them the
glorious, wonderful,
immaculate life of Jesus.

He found us weak, helpless and in all cases hopeless. He found us spiritually bankrupt, penniless. He found us, not only bankrupt but in debt to Him. Some of us lived in ignorance and others in open and willful rebellion. And what did He do with what He found? He placed His best robe around us, clothing us with Christ. He took His ring and placed it on our finger, adopting us as children and giving us His name. He slaughtered His best in order that we might feast. In short, He was outrageously extravagant when it came to our salvation. When we deserved nothing He extended compassion toward us and granted us mercy.

In the crowd stood a woman without significance. She was without a husband and most probably with children. We don't know much about her financial affairs, how well she handled what she had; whether or not she paid her bills on time, or even if she was a frequent "giver." But we know this: one day she came to give and the eyes of the Christ were upon her. She came to the place where the collection was being taken, opened her heart and her hand, and out dropped "two very small copper coins, worth only the fraction of a penny." "All she had to live on" the Savior commented.

I suppose many well-meaning brethren may have taken her aside and tried to convince her that God knew how much she needed what she had, and persuade her that she didn't need to give. I suppose they may have tried to convince her that she would be better off spending what she had on food, shelter or her children. I'm sure that some may even have lectured her on being a "wise steward," not understanding that this was the very thing she was being. For by her outrageous extravagance she not only won the approval and praise of the Christ but also won her place in the book of books, and in the hearts of all who have read her story.

Make no mistake about it, God commends such outrageous extravagance. And not only does He commend it, He commands it. In Matthew 19:21, Jesus deeply saddens a young man with the words, "If you want to be perfect, go, sell your possessions and give to the poor, and you will have treasure in heaven." Sadly, the young man chose to ignore the words of the Christ and we're told that he went away sorrowful because he had great wealth.

Now, if this were an isolated incident we may well be able to draw the conclusion that Jesus only said this to him *because* of his great wealth. However, in Luke 12:33, where the context describes the hearers as "little flock" (v. 32), or as "a crowd of many thousand" (v. 1), Jesus says the same thing again: "Sell your possessions and give to the poor. Provide purses for yourselves that will not wear out, a treasure in heaven that will not be exhausted, where no thief comes near and no moth destroys." Make no mistake, God commends and commands outrageous extravagance.

What will we say in reply to this? What will we do in response to God's outrageous extravagance toward us to bring about our salvation? What will we do about our Father's reaction to those who gave "all they had to live on"?

2 Corinthians 1:3-4

Praise be to the God and Father
of our Lord Jesus Christ,
the Father of compassion
and the God of all comfort,
who comforts us in all our troubles,
so that *we can comfort those in any trouble*
with the comfort we ourselves
have received from God.

The Biblical principle of blessing is that God does so, fully expecting those who are blessed to use it in the service of others. Our comfort, as the above text teaches, is meant to manifest itself in our lives through the comforting of others. Matthew 6:14 and 15 makes it abundantly clear that the mercy we receive should be demonstrated by our forgiving of others.

I read recently about a man, simply named Joe, who had had an alcohol problem. He was written off by the world and abandoned, as the weak regularly are. However, Joe struggled long and hard and finally got his problem under control, and decided to make effort toward making a difference, particularly among those of a similar ilk.

One afternoon outside the Mission Church, where Joe worked, lay a drunk. One of the attending Christians approached him and engaged in a little conversation, out of which blossomed the phrase, *"I wish I could be like Joe."* The Christian responded by saying, *"It would be better for you to hope to be like Jesus."* The drunk thought for a while and then said, *"Is He like Joe?"*

I absolutely love that. What a wonderful response. Whatever the drunk's shortcomings were, whatever his limitations involved, whatever else he knew, he knew this: If this Jesus character was anything like Joe, He was worth knowing. Whatever it was Joe was doing he was attracting strugglers and giving them hope . . . just like Jesus.

And what was Joe doing? Simply, extending compassion toward people because he himself had been shown compassion. Comforting as he himself had been comforted, and by all accounts he was surrounded . . . just like Jesus.

Peter, following the miraculous catch of fish, said, as he fell at the feet of Jesus, *"Go away from me, Lord. I am a sinful man."* Maybe it's just me, but isn't this a strange response to a haul of fish?

Peter was a fisherman. Catching fish was His livelihood. His whole world, the means by which he provided for his family, revolved around fishing. In this respect Jesus could not have blessed him more. Yet, at the receipt of such blessing Peter is reduced to his knees. Listen, and listen closely. We don't convince people of their need of forgiveness by shouting about their sin. We convince them by showing them the glorious, wonderful, immaculate life of Jesus. ("God's kindness leads to repentance"—true here and true always.)

William Barclay tells the story of a man who rode the train to work every day, and every day passed a little white cottage set against the lush greens and browns of the English countryside. He was constantly amazed at how white the cottage was, and how clean the people who lived there kept it. Then one day the snow fell all around, and the cottage was shown up for what it was; at best, gray.

Talk about sin all you like, but if people can't see the snow they have nothing to compare it against. Talk to them about Jesus and let the snow fall into their lives.

Peter is just one example; but the Scriptures, the Gospels in particular are bursting with examples of those who were renewed by the mercy of God. Their response to this is almost always uniform. They, to varying degrees, take God's lead and similarly proclaim and exhibit mercy.

The Karate Kid's opponent, Sensei John Kreese, informs his students that mercy is for the weak, a commonly held view. However, the only people who view mercy in this manner are those who have never been called to grant it to any great depth. Or, those who are unable or unwilling to.

Immediately following the "Road to Hell" where the allied troops pursued the Iraqi forces scampering from Kuwait they decided to hold back. Why? The word from the White House was that to continue the pursuit would end in a massacre and would be un-American. Although they would live to regret this because some years later they would be forced to engage in combat the very men they allowed to live, mercy was granted.

Without getting into any political issues here the granting of mercy toward those who in turn may even use the freedom provided to harm us is mercy of the highest standard, and noble beyond description. When God grants mercy His mind isn't troubled with the thought of those receiving it eventually turning against Him. He offers and grants it freely, to all.

The receipt of mercy lightens our hearts and brings gladness to our spirits. It releases the chains and casts off the burdens of guilt. In "Labelled with Love" by Difford and

Tilbrook, they tell a sad tale with a sorrowful ending phrase at the end of the chorus, "So the past has been bottled and labelled with love." The story is about a life gone wrong and anything that ever went right in it has been bottled and placed on the shelf like some kind of memento. However, this phrase in itself captures precisely the thought God would have seared in our hearts. Our past has been bottled and labeled with love.

On account of that, freed from our imprisonment, we seek to strive onward and upward to express the freedom and mercy we have received, doing all we can to portray in our little lives the majesty of what we have experienced in God. And to greater levels we must labor.

Oscar Schindler, a man declared to be a righteous person by the Council of Yad Vashem in Jerusalem for his part in saving so many Jewish lives during the time of the holocaust, was found distraught in the film that portrayed his life. He began his profiteering as the war began, using Jews as slave labor, viewing them as little more than a means to his most profitable end. However, as the years progressed his heart softened and his affections grew to the point were he bankrupted himself in efforts to save his "slaves."

There's an incredible scene at the end of the movie where Oscar is humbled by the gratitude of the Jewish workers, saved from the hell of Auschwitz. But it slowly begins to dawn on him that he could have done more. In response to the encouragement from the workers that he had done enough, he replied, "I could have done more." He stumbles as he cries, "This car. Why did I keep the car? There's ten people right there." He takes off his gold badge and weeps again,

"Here's another two." He said, "I wasted so much money. I could have saved more." In view of what Oscar did we may be inclined to agree with the Jewish workers that he did enough. That is, unless what he said was true: that he could have done more.

Let's not end our lives with these kinds of regrets. In view of God's outrageous extravagance toward our salvation let us mimic our Father in expressions of holy madness unparalleled since Acts 2:45.

The selling of our possessions in order that others may eat is commendable. The casting off of our pride, inhibitions and fear of future betrayal in order that others might receive and taste mercy is admirable and altogether Godlike.

CHAPTER 8

Zuzu's petals
THE RENEWAL OF ALL THINGS

There has never been a day,
and, there will never be a day,
where the Lord greets us without
renewed mercy for our souls.

Leaving everything in my wake, I bulleted down the road as fast as my legs could carry me, tears impairing my vision as I escaped the mad clutches of what can only be described as a sinister, malicious and depraved individual, seemingly hell-bent on inflicting as much pain as possible. Embarrassed, and two miles behind me, marched my pursuer. I can't remember how old I was but this is my earliest memory of a visit to the dentist.

I clearly recall being told that I was only there for a checkup and so I complied. However, two minutes into the "checkup" this masked maniac produced from behind his back a needle four-feet long (or so it seemed), and resembling an Olympic javelin champion began his run up to my mouth. Leaving a little cloud of dust on his seat I beat a hasty retreat.

Who would subject me to such torment? Who, in their right mind could possibly volunteer me for such cruelty? My mother, of course.

From kidding us into the dentist's chair to pouring antiseptic ointment on our scratches, *deep* into our wounds, mothers have an incredible capacity to hurt us. And it's not a conflict of interest with them. They do this willingly. It's not a lack of love that enables them to make such decisions and perform such torturous acts. It's an abundance of it. The momentary afflictions they are compelled to subject us to speak clearly of their over-riding desire to have us as healthy as we can possibly be, even at the expense of their becoming our objects of wrath.

Fathers on the other hand are different. They fulfill a different role. Among their many disguises is a banker, a comedian, a playmaker, and if we happen to be female, a chaperon-come-sniper, keeping watchful eye over all men who would dare to enter into the forbidden dating zone. But above that and what I suspect to be their holiest of callings, *they fix things*. That's what fathers do. Everything from broken toys to broken hearts are placed into the hands of our fathers in full expectation that given enough time, everything will be all right.

It's winter and children should be wrapping themselves up nice and warm. Zuzu, however, has a different agenda. She has a flower she doesn't want damaged. Consequently, at the expense of her health she makes sure the flower gets home safely. George Bailey arrives home to find his daughter in bed sick and goes up to her bedroom to check on her.

"Where do you think you're going?" George asks as Zuzu begins to make her way out of bed.

"I want to give my flower a drink."

George denies the request, proposing that he will give the flower the drink. Not surprisingly Zuzu is reluctant to part with her flower and in the tussle for the rose a few petals fall off.

"Look daddy," Zuzu says in the sweetest voice you ever heard in your life, and follows it closely with a plea, "Paste it."

You'll remember the scene well, I'm sure. George briefly turns his back on Zuzu, stuffs the few fallen petals into his pocket and presents the flower back to his daughter, good as new.

That's what fathers do! They fix things. Even when the limitations of their ability determine they are out of their depth, on they go, regardless, endeavoring to please their children and prove above all things, *I make things better*. They make broken things as new, to the delight of their little ones.

Talking of God, Jeremiah has this to say, *"Great is His faithfulness; His mercies begin afresh each day."*

There has never been a day, and, there will never be a day, where the Lord greets us without renewed mercy for our souls. His love for us compels Him, with every new day, to fully provide an abundance of mercy able to fulfill our requests.

This verse from Jeremiah is meant to mean something to us. That as the earth looks toward the east for the rising of the sun, so do our souls look toward our God for the rising of His mercy—each and every day. The beginning of each new day ought to be, in itself, a reminder to us that the mercy of God has been renewed.

Scientists will give us every explanation as to what makes a rainbow. They will break it down and tell us what it *really* is. Those who belong to God have little need for their explanations, for we already know what it is. It's a sign of a promise. A promise that our Father will never again destroy the earth by water.

God doesn't provide the rainbow to give us something nice to look at after the rain. He gives it to us to remind us of His promise, hoping beyond this, of course, that in seeing His faithfulness to *that* promise we would have reason to be confident in them all. So then, the rainbow becomes, not only a symbol of quiet waters, but also a beacon for the faithfulness of the One who made it.

So many things are like this in the Scriptures. They say things, that in and of themselves are good enough. But when we discover what they are *really* saying, the blinkers are removed, the curtains are opened, the light shines in and our hearts rejoice.

Here's Jesus surrounded by thousands of hungry people. We see Him take a few loaves and a couple of fish and from it produce an "all you can eat" buffet. We see this and we think, *"Wow He really impressed them there."* and undoubtedly He did. But is this all that it was? Not that I'm dissatisfied with the miracle, but if there's more to be said I'd like to hear it.

Doesn't Matthew 14 ring any bells? Doesn't it remind us of another wilderness in another place, where hungry multitudes were miraculously fed? This *isn't* just another miracle. There's a statement being made that would have sounded the bells in Israel. Jesus had compassion on these people and said, *"I have led you out into the wilderness and I have miraculously provided for you . . . Now, who am I?"* Yes, the writer of Hebrews was correct—someone greater than Moses was here.

The bread in the wilderness didn't sustain and nourish the Israelites. God did! The bread was only expressive of God Himself. Through the bread God was saying, "I am the Sustainer of life!" And, of course, Jesus would come along sometime later and say, *"I am the bread of life."*

The whole ministry of Jesus is supposed to speak to us of things, beyond that, which, on the face of it, are actually happening.

Prior to our fall in Genesis 3 there was no sickness, no disease and no death. As a direct result of the fall God brought all of these things upon us. Obviously the curse was a reaction to our rebellion, but we didn't curse ourselves.

God did. However, our sin resulted in more than a curse. It brought God to reverse the very things He had established in creation. The flood makes this abundantly clear.

At the creation God separated the waters from the land. At the flood He brought it all back in an act of un-creating.

In response to our rebellion, God chose, as a constant reminder to us, for the earth to rebel against us. No longer would she yield her fruit as freely as she once did, but by the sweat of our brows we would wrestle it from her.

He gave us health in the garden. In cursing us with pain, sickness and disease He was un-creating. He gave us life in the garden, and, with the introduction of death, He was, again, un-creating. But all of these things are served, not for the purpose of inflicting pain upon us, but with the intention of reminding us of the position we held and the height from which we had fallen. God wasn't endeavoring to make the punishment fit the crime, for if He did that we wouldn't be here at all. He was, as He *always* is, seeking our redemption. And everything in the curse is a reminder, a holy calling.

When we encounter pain, when we are confronted with death, when the thorn of a rose produces blood from our finger and when we witness the increased pain in childbearing we're meant to remember one thing: the garden. All of these things find their origin there.

Fast forward now, and watch as a young man from Nazareth walks among us, and treats these things as though they were nothing. Into a world of darkness, not unlike our Genesis, He brings forth light, and the blind can see. Sickness and disease are nothing to Him and the curse is reversed everywhere He goes. Demons and Satan himself are in subjection to Him, pathetically trying in vain to halt, or even hinder His progress. And when the earth, in her rebellious fashion, throws at Him a storm, He just carries on sleeping, until, that is, He is roused from His slumber. Twelve men, in fear and holy awe, tremble in the presence of the One who persuades the weather to think twice before knocking at His door. The earth is not in rebellion to this man; it's in submission.

Death terrifies us. Always has. For obvious reasons it turns the bravest into crumbling wrecks. And rightly so, for it is God's most vocal outrage at sin. Nowhere else is His point made so clearly, so seriously, and so completely. It's just so final. Well, it was until the Carpenter showed up.

To say that Jesus overcame and defeated death is a slur on His achievements. He didn't simply beat death, He utterly humiliated it. Annihilated it beyond all recognition. He beat it senseless, to a pulp, and as it lay whimpering on the floor, He grabbed it by the neck and held it up for all to see.

All that the Bible says about death is true. It truly is the greatest expression of God's holiness in response to sin. It's an ordeal that cannot be avoided and is to be dreaded, for it is recompense for our rebellion. However, one day a star came wandering and led us to a barn. Within the barn lay a child, not too unlike any other child, and yet. And yet.

When we consider Jesus, and witness His mighty acts, beyond being impressed by the power or the compassion, we're meant to notice that as far as the curse is concerned, in *HIM*, it has no effect.

All who came to Him had their bodies, their spirits, their faith, their lives, and more than this, renewed. But all of this, *all of it*, only spoke of what lies ahead: the renewal of all things. When we saw Jesus we witnessed firsthand a glimpse into the future. His ministry wasn't about what He could "perform" while He walked among us. It was meant to speak to us of a better day. A day when all things, in heaven and on earth, will be made new. A day when the curse will be, not momentarily lifted, but forever destroyed. *This* is what we must see in Jesus.

Those who place their faith in the Carpenter are in a state of constant recreation, which will one day manifest itself in an act of complete renewal. Understanding this we can deal with our momentary afflictions and in the face of it all proclaim, "It's a wonderful life!"

So, when our day comes, God willing, we'll meet it bravely. Why? For we have a Father in heaven whose pockets are bursting with our petals. He has made everything new. Now, and for always, everything is going to be all right. *"Bring me your broken lives,"* He calls to us. *"I'll fix them."*

After all, He's a Father—that's what they do.

Study Guide

"Bring me your
broken lives,"
He calls to us.
"I'll fix them."

CHAPTER 1 (In the beginning)

1. Are you a student of nature? Share a recent lesson you learned from a trip into God's creation.

    _____

    _____

    _____

2. Name some specific ways that you have limited yourself in your own comfortable world.

    _____

    _____

    _____

3. What is the difference between life and abundant life?

    _____

    _____

    _____

4. What area of the world declares God's glory most to you? Why?

    _____

    _____

    _____

    _____

5. When is it legitimate to be discontent with our lives?

    _____

    _____

    _____

6. How has this chapter inspired you to desire a new beginning?

    _____

    _____

    _____

CHAPTER 2 (There's more than this)

1. In 2 Corinthians 4:16, Paul encourages the readers not to lose heart. What is it about faith that enables us in this regard?

    _____

    _____

    _____

2. What do you think is meant by the words, "When it all boils down, it boils down to faith"?

    _____

    _____

    _____

3. Why are "faith" and "sight" so at odds with each other?

    _____

    _____

    _____

    _____

4. Why do you think faith is so important to God, and why is it so appealing to Him?

   _____

   _____

   _____

5. How do you think the world is so convincing when it comes to persuading us to depend upon it?

   _____

   _____

   _____

6. What problems are surrounding you at this time? What steps do you think you need to take to remedy the problems?

   _____

   _____

   _____

CHAPTER 3 (Blessed are the lunatics)

1. Discuss a time when you have been considered a fool by the world because of your faith.

   _____

   _____

   _____

   _____

2. Why do you think the world struggles with understanding Christianity, when it appears to us so simple?

   _____

   _____

   _____

3. This chapter mentions "making room for God." How is
    this achieved?

    _____

    _____

    _____

4. Has there ever been a time when you've received some
    flak from your church family for getting out of the boat?
    How did you deal with that?

    _____

    _____

    _____

5. What things in your life do you think you'll pack onto Jesus
    with a certain amount of joy and sense of achievement?

    _____

    _____

    _____

6. For what area(s) of your life do you need to be buying
    bigger frying pans?

    _____

    _____

    _____

CHAPTER 4 (I saw God today)

1. Where in creation do you see God clearest of all?

    _____

    _____

    _____

2. Why do you think we struggle so much with finding time to spend in the Word? What can we do to change this?

_____

_____

_____

3. Off the top of your head, how many incidents can you list where God chose ordinary things/people to accomplish extraordinary results?

_____

_____

_____

_____

4. Psalm 119:100—What is it about obedience that brings understanding?

_____

_____

_____

5. What talents/gifts do you already possess that God could use in His service?

_____

_____

_____

6. What particular gift would you like God to bless you with, and why?

_____

_____

_____

CHAPTER 5 (Let the ballerina dance)

1. What possessions do you have that are simply irreplaceable?

   _____

   _____

   _____

2. What aspect of God attracts you to Him more than any
   other, and why?

   _____

   _____

   _____

3. What practical steps can we take to ensure that our homes
   become environments where God can be found with ease?

   _____

   _____

   _____

4. What does it mean to you to "seek first His kingdom and
   His righteousness"?

   _____

   _____

   _____

5. How can we ensure we don't drift into either of the
   extremes mentioned in this chapter?

   _____

   _____

   _____

6. Discuss a time when you felt the hand of God around your waist.

_____

_____

_____

CHAPTER 6 (I would be delighted)

1. What delights you most in this world? Supply two answers here: one spiritual and one physical.

_____

_____

_____

2. How does God's delight in showing mercy motivate you, and how does it prompt you to behave?

_____

_____

_____

3. Considering the debt that has been canceled on our behalf, why do you think we struggle so much to forgive others?

_____

_____

_____

4. What do you think the church should be striving to be known for within our communities?

_____

_____

_____

5. What lessons do we learn from the woman at Simon the Pharisee's house?

    _____

    _____

    _____

6. What can we do to make ourselves more appealing to the un-forgiven?

    _____

    _____

    _____

CHAPTER 7 (Labeled with love)

1. Has there ever been a time when you have given "all you had to live on"? What was the result?

    _____

    _____

    _____

2. In what ways are you using the blessings God has given to you to bless others?

    _____

    _____

    _____

3. "God's kindness leads to repentance"—if this is true, how ought this to manifest itself in our lives?

    _____

    _____

    _____

4. Have you ever had the mercy you've granted come back and bite you? How did you feel? How did you deal with it?

    _____

    _____

    _____

5. What lessons do we learn from Oscar Schindler?

    _____

    _____

    _____

6. How does the erasing of our pasts help us deal with the future?

    _____

    _____

    _____

CHAPTER 8 (Zuzu's petals)

1. Which movie has truly helped you in your walk with God, and why?

    _____

    _____

    _____

2. List some things your parents forced you to do, which, as children, you thought to be severe, but later understood to be loving.

    _____

    _____

    _____

3.   What do you think about when you see a rainbow?

_____

_____

_____

4.   Discuss something you found in Scripture that you
     thought to be "simple," but when it was fully explained
     just thrilled your soul.

_____

_____

_____

5.   What do the extreme measures of the curse have to say
     to us about ourselves and about God?

_____

_____

_____

6.   What do you believe you'll think of your trials here on
     earth once you finally arrive in heaven?

_____

_____

_____

_____

About the Author

Contact information:
Billy Wilson
39 Croftfoot Road
Glasgow G44 5JS
Scotland

E-mail: WilsonRFC@aol.com

If you have any comments I would be pleased to hear them. If you have any questions I will gladly do my best to answer them. If you have a beach home in the Caribbean I would gladly stay there.

Part of my ministry includes writing and recording gospel albums. If you would be interested in these they can be ordered from the above e-mail address.

Finally, a prayer request:

It is our intention to move to Holywood, Northern Ireland, at the beginning of 2005, to minister alongside Jim McGuiggan. We are in the process of making plans and raising the necessary funds to accomplish this. Please bring this to our Father on our behalf. Thank you.